GROWING IN

G000088560

Was Jesus Christ a Mere Human?

Were the Ebionites Correct?

Michael Harvey Koplitz

Michael Harvey Koplitz

All Scripture quotations, unless otherwise noted, are taken from the New American Standard Bible®, Copyright © 1960, 1962, 1963, 1968, 1971, 1972, 1973, 1975, 1977, 1995 by the Lockman Foundation. Used by permission. (www.Lockman.org)

The NASB uses italic to indicate words that have been added for clarification. Citations are shown with large capital letters.

Published by Michael H. Koplitz

ISBN-13: 9798634601076

Table of Contents

**THE LARGE MARGINS ARE INTENTIONAL.
THEY ARE FOR YOUR NOTES (ONLY
AVAILABLE IN THE PAPERBACK EDITION)**

Michael Harvey Koplitz

ACKNOWLEDGMENTS

This work could not have been accomplished without Dr. Anne Davis, who taught me Ancient (Hebraic) Bible study methods, and my two study partners, Rev. Dr. Robert Cook and Pastor Sandra Koplitz. We know that the journey has just started and will last a lifetime. The discovery of the depths of God's Word is waiting for us to find.

Michael Harvey Koplitz

Introduction

Matt. 20:23 He said to them, "My cup you shall drink; but to sit on My right and on *My* left, this is not Mine to give, but it is for those for whom it has been prepared by My Father."

Some questions arise when reading the Scripture, especially when using Ancient Bible Study Methods.[1] If you are not familiar with this method, a chapter about the difference between Greek/Western learning methods and Hebraic methods is included. Ancient Methods is Hebraic methods with the addition of the culture and the language of Jesus' day. The

---

[1] If you do not know Ancient Bible Study methods the author has published several books on this topic. You can also find information at his website, http://michaelkoplitz.info.

result is an interpretation of the Scripture the way Jesus and His followers understood it. The church has placed filters on the Scripture, telling us for centuries what to believe. The Catholic Church forbade catholic Christians from owning a Bible until 1964 CE. By doing this Catholic Church prevented its membership from discovering what Jesus said and did for themselves.

It is passages like Matthew 20:23, which arise in the synoptic Gospels (Matthew, Mark, and Luke) that bring up a concern about how the disciples viewed Jesus and how Jesus viewed Himself. Did the disciples think that Jesus was God? The answer is probably not. Bart Ehrman wrote an excellent book titled "How Jesus Became God: The Exaltation of a Jewish Preacher from Galilee." This book is one of several other books that ask and offer possibilities to this question. Somewhere between 40 CE and 90 CE is when the Proto-Orthodox church declared Jesus as God.

Matthew 20:23 is one of several passages in the synoptic Gospels that Jesus tells us directly that He is not God. What about John's Gospel? That book was written after 90 CE, especially for the Proto-Orthodox church. By then, this emerging church, which dominated all its competitors, believed that Jesus was God. John's Gospel expresses the Proto-Orthodox church's view of Jesus.

A reason for the Proto-Orthodox church's belief in Jesus as God came from its origins being in the Mithras cult. In the ancient world, it was common for people to change their allegiance from one god to another god. Paul was a good convincer. When Paul left Damascus and made his travels around the Roman world, he converted Mithras house churches. The Mithras cult had many different names throughout history. By Roman times the cult's "leader" was Mithras. Paul entered these house churches and convinced them that Mithras was not their God, but rather Jesus of Nazareth was. The ideas of baptism, communion, and other facets of Christianity's doctrine and ritual come directly from Mithras.[2]

Mithras was the son of god who died for the sins of people. He was born to a virgin, and

---

[2] The author wrote a book titled "Christianity's Need for Mithras" which discusses the conversion of Mithras house churches into Jesus house churches.

Mithras will come again. There are more areas of doctrine that connect Mithras to Christianity. It is well documented that the faith picked up believes from pagan cultures and made them a part of the Christian faith. Poinsettias, Christmas trees, and lilies at Easter are just some examples.

The Proto-Orthodox church, based on the Mithras house churches, changed their god from Mithras to Jesus. Paul did interject some of the morals and ethics of Judaism into the churches. This interjection can be seen in Paul's letters to the churches which are found in the New Testament. A lot of the discussions are about morals and ethics.

I have written two other books about the possible origin of Jesus of Nazareth and His relationship to the LORD. The first one was the postulation that Jesus of Nazareth was a teraphim angel sent as the Messiah. The second was the postulation that Jesus was either the Sefirah Tiferet or the angel of the Sefirah Tiferet.

This is the third postulation. Could the Ebionites have been partially correct? Their doctrine was that Jesus of Nazareth was human-like anyone of us. He followed the LORD's commandments to the letter. After His death, the LORD raised him from the dead and exalted Him to become divine. The last part is what this paper does not agree with, and it will be shown why.

So the investigation is, was Jesus, just another human who followed the commandments of the LORD.

Michael Harvey Koplitz

Before you start reading

I have been using Ancient Bible Study Methods developed initially by the Sage Hillel to analyze Scripture for many years. I learned the Greek/Western method of Scripture analysis while attending Seminary. I found that the Greek/Western process did not explain many of the events in the New Testament. Using a Hebraic approach to a Hebraic document has been opening up a deeper understanding of the LORD's Word. I have incorporated the culture of Jesus' day and His native language, Aramaic, to expand the analysis of biblical passages.

The LORD's Word contains various depths of understanding. The rabbis say that there are at least seventy depths of understanding to the

Torah. Why? Because a person will hear the Torah read at least that many times in their lives. The synagogue reads the Torah through each year.

What is presented here is an understanding of Jesus of Nazareth, using the synoptic Gospels, as a human. When you read this presentation, take note that I am not saying that this is what I believe nor what you should believe. It is an academic presentation.

In Hebraic studies, anything can be debated as long as the premise of the discussion is biblical. What is presented is biblical. Some readers will have difficulty reading this presentation because of what the church has taught them. The debate is not about the church being incorrect or not. It is a presentation of looking at the life of Jesus of Nazareth using the synoptic Gospels. If you feel that you will get angered by such a presentation, then I advise you to stop reading right now.

Hebraic studies allow for the free expression of ideas. Remember that none of us have a clear answer to the theological questions of the world. This statement is true because of the numerous religious expressions that exist in the world. Christianity today has many expressions. Today they have labels like Methodists, Lutherans, Catholics, and many more. Also, we have a new label for some churches, the independent churches. These independent churches develop what they want their theological position to be.

So if you are still reading this book, then you are open to reading something extremely different then what the church professes as the understanding of Jesus of Nazareth.

One last statement is that I am NOT saying that this is my theological position. I am presenting a possibility that is worth contemplating. That is all. Now, if you are ready and have an open mind, please continue to the introduction or the next chapter.

The main differences between the Greek method and the Hebraic method of teaching

Once a student becomes aware of these two teaching styles, the student will be able to determine if the class attended or if a book read, whether the teaching method is either a Greek or Hebraic method. In the Greek manner, the instructor is always right because of advanced knowledge. In the college situation, it is because the professor has his/her Ph.D. in some area of study, so one assumes that he or she knows everything about the topic. For example, Rodney Dangerfield played the role of a middle-aged man going to college. His English midterm was to write about Kurt Vonnegut Jr. Since he did not understand any of Vonnegut's books, he

19

hired Vonnegut himself to write the midterm. When he received the paper from the English Professor told Dangerfield that whoever wrote the paper knew nothing about Vonnegut. The professor's words are an example of the Greek method of teaching. Did the Ph.D. English professor think that she knew more about Vonnegut's writings than Vonnegut did? [3]

In the Greek teaching method, the professor or the instructor claims to be the authority. If one attends a Bible study class and the class leader says, "I will teach you the only way to understand this biblical book," you may want to consider the implications. This method is standard since most Seminaries and Bible

---

[3] *Back to School*. Performed by Rodney Dangerfield.
        Hollywood: CA: Paper Clip Productions, 1986. DVD.

colleges teach a Greek mode of learning, which is the same method the church has been utilizing for centuries.

Hebraic teaching methods are different. The teacher wants the students to challenge what they hear. It is through questioning that a student can learn. Also, the teacher wants his/her students to excel to a point where the student becomes the teacher.

If two rabbis come together to discuss a passage of Scripture, the result will be at least ten different opinions. All points of view are acceptable if each is supported by biblical evidence. It is permissible and encouraged that students develop many ideas. There is a depth to God's Word, and God wants us to find all His messages contained in the Scripture.

Seeking out the meaning of the Scriptures beyond the literal meaning is essential to understand God's Word fully.[4] The Greek method of learning the Scriptures has prevailed over the centuries. One problem is that only the literal interpretation of Scripture was often viewed as valid, as prompted by Martin Luther's "sola literalis" meaning that just the literal translation of Scripture was accurate. The Fundamentalist movements of today base their beliefs on the literal interpretation of the Scripture. Therefore, they do not believe that

---

[4] Davis, Anne Kimball. *The Synoptic Gospels*. MP3. Albuquerque: NM: BibleInteract, 2012.

God placed more profound, hidden, or secret meanings in the Word.

The students of the Scriptures who learn through Hebraic training and understanding have drawn a different conclusion. The Hebrew language itself leads to different possible interpretations because of the construction of the language. The Hebraic method of Bible study opens avenues of thought about God's revelations in the Scripture never considered. Not all questions about the Scripture studied will have an immediate answer. If so, it becomes the responsibility of the learners to uncover the meaning. Also, remember that many opinions about the meaning of Scripture are also acceptable.

Michael Harvey Koplitz

Who were the Ebionites, and what did they believe?

Simply stated, the Ebionites were a group that followed the ways of Jesus of Nazareth, believing that He was the Messiah but not God. You will not hear about them in your local church because they were declared a heresy by the Proto-Orthodox church when it grew large enough to grab power. The Proto-Orthodox church destroyed all other forms of Christianity. Once that was accomplished, the Proto-Orthodox Church became the only sanctioned church in the Roman Empire.

Unfortunately, the Proto-Orthodox church destroyed the documents and records of all its competitors. The Gnostics, who believed that Jesus of Nazareth brought the Secret Word of God, which Moses received on Mount Sinai and was lost over the centuries, survived and is in publication today. The Gnostics placed their writings in jars that ended up in the garbage dump at Alexandria Egypt. They were discovered in 1948 and have been studied and read ever since then. The Proto-Orthodox church snuffed them out in the second century CE.

There were other Christian movements that the Proto-Orthodox church destroyed. Unfortunately, we will never have their writings. The Catholic and Orthodox churches have decided that everything their leadership decides is not beneficial to them a heresy. Many people have died over the centuries because their objections to the church were declared heresy.

In 1517 the Reformation began, and Martin Luther's writing was not destroyed. He was told to recant his theological position as heresy. He refused, and that sparked the ready to explode church. If the printing press was not invented seventy years earlier, none of Luther's theological ideas would have survived.

What about the Ebionites? There are people in Christian churches today who do not believe that Jesus of Nazareth was God incarnated. The church does not hunt them down as it did 1900 years ago. However, when they are discovered, they are usually escorted out.

27

The Ebionite theology that this research paper question is the belief that Jesus of Nazareth was made divine after his death. The idea of a resurrection was fresh in the Near East. This idea came with the Greek and the introduction of Hellenism. It was a new concept that had believers and opponents.

If the idea of the separation of the spirit and body is real, then when each human dies, their spirit will separate from their body and will return to God. The only difference between Jesus of Nazareth is what happened after the resurrection.

The custom of the day was to return to a grave on the third day after death. It was believed that the visitors to the grave could be heard by the deceased. One would be saying their final goodbyes. The difference with Jesus of Nazareth is that it is believed that he was seen that day and several times afterward for forty days. The historian Josephus notes in his writing that Jesus of Nazareth was seen after his death.

That does not mean that Jesus was divine. It does mean that his spirit could be heard and possibly seen before he departed the Earth.

Michael Harvey Koplitz

The Resurrection Events

The synoptic Gospels disagree with what happened on the third day after Jesus' death. If the three Gospels are compared to John's Gospel, there are a lot of interesting points to explore.

In Matthew's Gospel, Jesus instructs the women at the grave to tell the disciples to meet Him in the Galilee later that day. However, the disciples are in Jerusalem. It was not physically possible for the eleven remaining disciples to travel from Jerusalem, where the crucifixion occurred to the Galilee. That was a seven-day journey. However, Matthew's Gospel says that Jesus met his disciples in the Galilee the night of the third day. That timeline just does not work. Also, Matthew's Gospel says that Jesus ascended to Heaven right there. Jesus left behind what is called the Great Commission.

Mark's Gospel had nothing after Jesus' death. Later on, after the writing of this Gospel, several verses were added to the end of the book. Jesus meets with his disciples on the third day to give them instructions and then ascends to heaven.

Luke's Gospel has several times that Jesus appears to one or more of his disciples after His resurrection. Eventually, he ascends to Heaven. The Book of Acts is supposed to be a continuation of Luke's Gospel. However, Acts commences with Jesus' ascension, which is different in Luke when compared to Acts. Which is correct? The idea that the same author penned both books does not fly because of the apparent differences in the same story.

John's Gospel was written to comply with the new Proto-Orthodox church's beliefs. Since this flavor of Christianity was based on the Mithras cult, one can see Mithras in John's Gospel. There are several events of the post-Jesus resurrection. The big difference with the other Gospels is that John's Gospel says that Jesus gave the disciples the Holy Spirit that evening. In the current Orthodox church, the belief is that the Father and the Son created the Holy Spirit that night. Well, that is interesting because, at the beginning of John's Gospel, the Holy Spirit comes upon Jesus when John baptized him in the Jordan River.

So did the women see Jesus, or did they feel him with them and imagined the physical appearance. Alternatively, was the resurrection stories of Jesus added to the Gospels when the Proto-Orthodox church took control of the writings. Mithras resurrected from the dead three days after his death. If Jesus replaced Mithras, then Jesus had to rise from the grave on the third day after his death.

Jesus' Baptism

Jesus came to the river Jordan where his cousin was performing the mikvah ritual. This cleansing was for the forgiveness of sins. The people believed that the LORD forgave sins through the mikvah, which enabled poor Jews to atone for their sins. The church states that Jesus was without any sin. Since Jesus grew up from an infant to a man, he probably disobeyed his parents along the way. In Luke's Gospel, there is a narrative of the family being in Jerusalem. After leaving, Jesus' parents discovered that he was not with the caravan. They found Jesus in the Temple, discussing the Bible with the priests. Jesus is told in that passage that he sinned against his parents. The church insists that Jesus did not sin. However, the Infancy Gospel of Thomas has narratives in it where the young Jesus does sin.

Young kids sin by not obeying their parents. Every generation since the human model was introduced had children disobeying parents. It is expected that children will test the boundaries to learn and grow. Jesus would have done this also.

Therefore, Jesus wanted to go through the mikvah in order to cleanse himself of these childhood sins before he could start his messianic ministry. If Jesus were God incarnate, then he would have never disobeyed his parents.

The Holy Spirit sends Jesus into the desert

If Trinity doctrine is correct, why does the Holy Spirit lead Jesus into the desert? The Holy Spirit would just think "go to the desert," and the Son would go. Being three in one, if the Holy Spirit were thinking about it, then certainly the Son would know of it. The Gospels say that Jesus is directed into the desert by the Holy Spirit.

Mark 1:12 Immediately the Spirit impelled Him *to go* out into the wilderness. [13] And He was in the wilderness forty days being tempted by Satan; and He was with the wild beasts, and the angels were ministering to Him.

Michael Harvey Koplitz

Not knowing things

One area that the Gospels bring up is when Jesus will return. The concept comes from the Mithras cult and becomes incorporated in Christianity because Paul converted to Christianity the Mithras house churches. The real question is not will Jesus return, but rather Jesus says that he does not know when he would return. If Jesus was God incarnate, how can he not know when he will return? Jesus said in the Gospels that only the Father knows the time. If Trinity doctrine is true, then whatever the Father knows the Son and Holy Spirit know. One part of the Trinity cannot hide information that is contained in the Godhead. All three would share information.

So, how can Jesus be called the Son, a part of the Godhead, and not know what the plans of God are? Logic says that this does not work.

A church explanation is that Jesus divested himself of his divinity when he came to Earth. This process can be found in Philippians chapter two and is called Kenosis. Paul's theology is that when Jesus came down to Earth that he left his divinity in Heaven. When he ascended to Heaven, he regained it. Some events are recorded in the Gospels that the church says indicates that Jesus had divine healing powers while on Earth. The church points out that Jesus was not a physician, but instead, he performed miracle healings. If so, then Paul is incorrect, and Jesus did bring his divinity with him. If so, then he knew when he was to return.

There is a bit of confusion when placing several Gospel stories together about whether or not Jesus had divine knowledge and power. The disciples of Jesus did not see him as God incarnate. They did see him as the Messiah whom the LORD promised to send to Israel. There is a big difference between being God incarnate and being the Messiah promised.

Matt. 24:36 "But *a*of that day and hour no one knows, not even the angels of Heaven, nor the Son, but the Father alone. [37] "For [1]the *a*coming of the Son of Man will be *b*just like the days of Noah. [3]

Michael Harvey Koplitz

Jesus birth

Jesus' birth in Bethlehem is puzzling because of the predictions found in the minor prophets about the Day of the LORD. This understanding is one of the reasons that Jews have a difficult time accepting Jesus as the Messiah. The prophecies of the Messiah do not indicate that the Messiah is the LORD returning to Earth. When the Proto-orthodox church decided that Jesus was God incarnate, Jews had a difficult time accepting this concept.

Why? Because the minor prophets said that when the LORD returns, the Day of the LORD will be invoked. The Day of the LORD is the end of time. Judgment would occur across the Earth. Evil people would be removed from the

Earth, and the righteous people would rule. Eventually, a new Heaven and new Earth would be formed where evil does not exist.

When Jesus was born, the Day of the LORD did not happen. According to Luke's Gospel, there was fanfare and rejoicing because the Messiah was born. Luke does not say that God incarnate was born. He says that the Messiah was born. The early church in Jerusalem, composed mainly of Jews, viewed Jesus as the Messiah. They continued to bring their offerings for the forgiveness of sin to the Temple at Jerusalem. The concept of Jesus as God who died to forgive all sins was not a part of the Jerusalem church. Around 90 CE, that group of Christians disappeared from history.

The converted Mithras house churches were flourishing and banned together to become the Proto-orthodox church. Mithras was god incarnate. Mithras was going to return. Mithras died for the forgiveness of sins for the world. Mithras required baptism. Mithras had a communion ritual almost identical to the church. The converted Mithras house church declared Jesus of Nazareth God, the substitute for Mithras.

This substitution happened because Paul went north and west, telling Mithras churches that they were worshiping the wrong God. Jesus took the place of Mithras. Jesus became known to Proto-Orthodox Christians as God. Any group that claimed to believe in the Messiahship of Jesus but not the divinity of Jesus was quickly snuffed out by the Proto-Orthodox church.

Luke 2 [4] Joseph also went up from Galilee, from the city of Nazareth, to Judea, to the city of David which is called Bethlehem, because [a]he was of the house and family of David, [5] in order to register along with Mary, who was engaged to him, and was with child. [6] While they were there, the days were completed for her to give birth. [7] And she [a]gave birth to her firstborn Son; and she wrapped Him in cloths, and laid Him in a [1]manger, because there was no room for them in the inn. [8] In the same region there were *some* shepherds staying out in the fields and keeping watch over their flock by night. [9] And [a]an angel of the Lord suddenly [b]stood before them, and the glory of the Lord shone around them; and they were terribly frightened. [10] But the angel said to them,

""*Do not be afraid; for behold, I bring you good news of great joy which will be for all the people; ¹¹ for today in the city of David there has been born for you a *Savior, who is ¹*Christ ʿthe Lord. ¹² ""*This *will be* a sign for you: you will find a baby wrapped in cloths and lying in a ¹manger."

Michael Harvey Koplitz

Conclusion

There are numerous examples in the synoptic Gospels that point to Jesus being a mere human being. The Jewish-Christians in Judea and the Galilee kept bringing sacrifices to the Temple in Jerusalem until it was destroyed in 70 CE. Why would they continue to do this if Jesus died for their sins and was a God? If the writings of the Jerusalem Church had survived, we would have an answer to that question and many more.

Paul's house churches were converted Mithras churches. The evidence is clear on this question. So, Jesus of Nazareth was made a God when Paul substituted Jesus for Mithras. For that form of Christianity, Jesus was a God. For the other early forms of Christianity, He was not.

Jesus was followed like any other rabbi. He was an outstanding teacher who said some incredibly profound remarks during his lifetime. His understanding of what the LORD wanted from people was insightful and extraordinary. Jesus followed the LORD's way and spoke the LORD's word up to and including His time on the cross.

Jesus' reward was His being exalted in Heaven. His life was one of service to others. He died to demonstrate to us that what He said was truly from the LORD. He walked his talk and never swayed from it.

Whether Jesus was God incarnate or not, Jesus' method for living a godly life of high ethics and morals is the way to be an excellent member of society. If everyone in the world followed Jesus' words and actions, this place would become the Kingdom of God.

You do not have to attend a church to be a disciple of Jesus. Churches did not exist in Jesus' day. Worship and praise to the LORD for all blessings is a part of following the ways of Jesus. Do not restrict yourself to one kind of way of understanding Jesus.

Whether Jesus was a mere human or God incarnate should not take away from the prestigious life one can have by following Jesus' way.

Michael Harvey Koplitz

Bibliography

1986. *Back to School.*

Davis, Anne Kimball. 2012. *The Symoptic Gospels.* Comp. Anne Kimball Davis.

Printed in Great Britain
by Amazon